THE WORLD'S GREATEST
BABY FARM ANIMALS
Poster Book

Voyageur Press

First published in 2008 by Voyageur Press, an imprint of MBI Publishing Company LLC, Galtier Plaza, Suite 200, 380 Jackson Street, St. Paul, MN 55101 USA

The information in this book is true and complete to the best of our knowledge. All recommendations are made without any guarantee on the part of the author or Publisher, who also disclaim any liability incurred in connection with the use of this data or specific details.

We recognize, further, that some words, model names, and designations mentioned herein are the property of the trademark holder. We use them for identification purposes only. This is not an official publication.

Voyageur Press titles are also available at discounts in bulk quantity for industrial or sales-promotional use. For details write to Special Sales Manager at MBI Publishing Company, Galtier Plaza, Suite 200, 380 Jackson Street, St. Paul, MN 55101 USA.

To find out more about our books, join us online at www.voyageurpress.com.

Library of Congress Cataloging-in-Publication Data

Johnson, Samantha.
  The world's greatest baby farm animals poster book / by Samantha Johnson ; photography by Daniel Johnson.
    p. cm.
  ISBN-13: 978-0-7603-3330-3 (softbound)
  1. Domestic animals—Infancy—Pictorial works.
I. Johnson, Daniel, 1984– II. Title.
SF76.J64 2008
636'.07—dc22
                                    2007043019

About the author: Daniel Johnson specializes in equine photography, but he also enjoys photographing many other subjects, such as dogs, farm animals, gardens, and rural life. Dan also manages the family-owned horse farm and oversees the breeding, training, and showing of their horses. He lives in Phelps, Wisconsin.

Samantha Johnson is a certified horse show judge and a freelance writer. Her articles have appeared in many horse-centric magazines. She also works at Fox Hill Farm and specializes in foaling. She lives in Phelps, Wisconsin.

All photos by Daniel Johnson except on pages 32, 41, 44, 52, 57, and 64. Those photos are by Norvia Behling.

Title page: *Daniel Johnson*
On the cover: *Daniel Johnson*
On the back cover: *Daniel Johnson*

Editor: Amy Glaser
Designer: Brenda C. Canales

Printed in China

Cria Baby

A baby llama is called a cria (pronounced cree-ah). Crias weigh less than thirty pounds at birth, and they come in many colors and color combinations. As with many other large farm animals, such as horses and cows, baby llamas are usually born one at a time, and twins are extremely rare.

Llama Fun Fact

Llamas are now very popular on farms in North America, but they originally came from South America. Llamas are similar to camels in many ways and were historically used as pack animals. Today many people enjoy them as pets, but they are also used as livestock guardians, and some are raised for their wool.

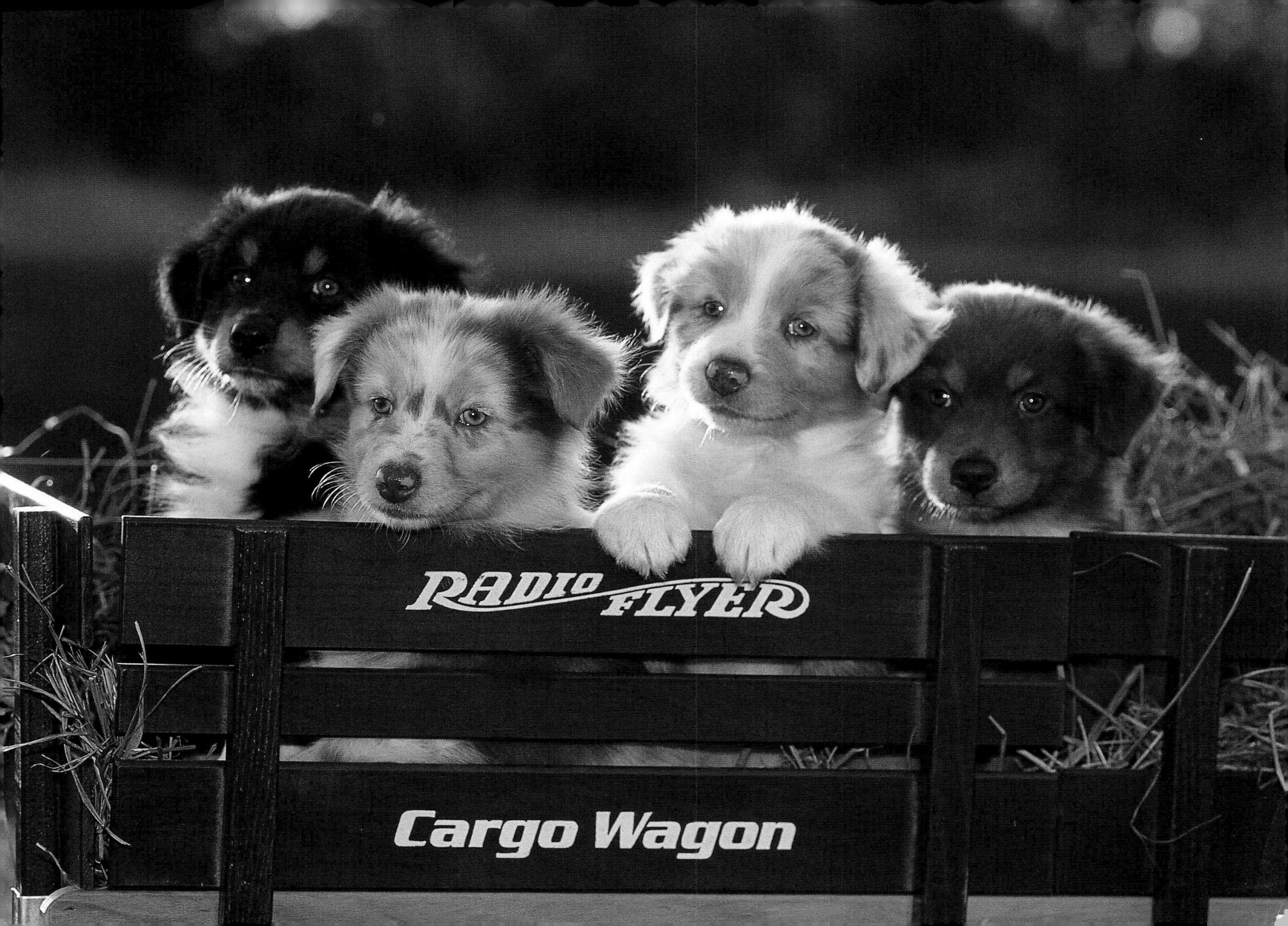
RADIO FLYER
Cargo Wagon

Puppy Pals

What's more fun than a wagon full of puppies? These adorable Australian shepherd puppies are eight weeks old. Even though they are different colors and have different markings, they are all from the same litter. The puppy on the left is a black tri-color, the two puppies in the middle have red merle coloring, and the puppy on the right is a solid red. The red merle puppies have white blazes on their faces.

Puppy Fun Fact

Puppies are born with their eyes closed and are deaf and helpless. They do not venture outside of their "nest" until their eyes open, which does not happen until the puppies are 12 to 15 days old. They gain their sense of hearing at about the same time. After their eyes and ears are open, they quickly become rolling, romping little rascals.

Saanen Goats

There are different types of goats for different purposes, including fiber, meat, and dairy goats. These inquisitive goat kids are Saanen goats, a type of dairy goat. The Saanen breed is of Swiss origin, and the goats are larger than some of the other dairy goat breeds, standing up to 35 inches tall.

Goat Fun Fact

Like some other types of mammals, including rabbits and deer, adult male goats are known as bucks, and adult female goats are known as does. However, baby rabbits are called kits and baby deer are called fawns, while baby goats are known as kids. Baby goats are popular on farms where human kids love to play with goat kids!

Miniature Mule

His father is a donkey, his mother is a miniature horse, so what does that make this adorable foal? He's a miniature mule, of course! This little fellow will be less than 50 inches tall when mature, yet he maintains some of the characteristics of his donkey heritage, including the long ears!

Miniature Mule Fun Fact
Mules come in many sizes, including draft mules, which are giant creatures that can be more than 17 hands tall! Miniature mules have a miniature horse parent, which is why they are so much smaller. Many people enjoy their miniature mules because of their diminutive size and other irresistible charms.

Beef Calves

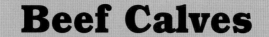

There are many different breeds of beef cattle, and each has many different characteristics. For instance, the Angus breed is characterized by black coloring, the Scottish Highland has long horns, and the Hereford is red with a white face. Like goats, some breeds of cattle are horned and some are polled (do not have horns).

Calf Fun Fact

These young calves have one parent that is an Angus and one parent that is a Hereford. It's interesting to see that the dark calf looks more like an Angus than a Hereford, while the other calf inherited the black coloring from the Angus and the white face from the Hereford.

Kitty Litter

These five kittens are from the same litter, even though they look very different. Kittens from the same litter are often different colors. Litters typically consist of 2 to 5 kittens, but the largest litter ever recorded consisted of 19 kittens!

Kitten Fun Fact

Kittens are born after approximately 60 to 67 days of gestation. Like puppies, kittens are born blind and deaf. Their eyes do not open until after they are at least a week old, and their sense of hearing is not well developed for about two weeks.

Mares and Foals

What is cuter than a mare and her foal? Mares are extremely protective of their newborn foals and keep them by their side at all times. They can even become slightly aggressive to other horses who venture too close to the new arrival. As the foal grows older, the mare becomes more relaxed and allows her baby to explore the paddock and begin interacting with other horses.

Foal Fun Fact

Newborn foals nurse for approximately five minutes every half-hour. The need for such constant nursing diminishes as the foal grows older and begins grazing and eating other foods. By the time a foal is three months old, he or she nurses once every few hours, and this continues to decrease with age. Foals are typically weaned between the ages of three and eight months.

Guard Puppy

This four-month-old puppy is a future farm dog. His father was a Great Pyrenees, a breed that is noted for its excellent livestock guard dogs. They protect the farm animals from predators. This puppy's mother was a collie, another breed that is popular with farm families. Collies are loving and kind dogs that thrive on work and attention. This puppy should become a wonderful farm dog and maintain these qualities from each breed.

Puppy Fun Fact

The Great Pyrenees breed originated in France and is named for the Pyrenean Mountains in France. The dogs are well known for their courage and intelligence. Great Pyrenees dogs have proved their devotion and loyalty for centuries by guarding the livestock and protecting the farm. They are also extremely large and can be as tall as 32 inches.

Mary Had a Little Lamb

This adorable lamb is six weeks old. Lambs nurse frequently during their first few weeks of life, and the frequency decreases as the lamb gets older. Lambs should not be weaned before they are six weeks old, and many farmers believe it should be delayed until the lamb is at least three months old.

Lamb Fun Fact
In order to keep track of which lambs belong to which ewes, farmers will mark the lambs with a number that corresponds to a number marked on their mothers. That way the farmer always knows to whom each lamb belongs.

Nigerian Dwarf Goats

These adorable goat kids are Nigerian dwarf goats, a miniature type of dairy goat. Nigerian dwarf goats are found in many different colors, including white, as shown here. Nigerian dwarfs are popular on farms because of their small size and impressive milk production. Farmers also make cheese and soap from goat's milk.

Goats Fun Fact

Play time! These rambunctious twins illustrate the fact that the Nigerian Dwarf usually produces more than one kid at a time—sometimes as many as five at once! These kids are enjoying a playful romp together in the grass.

Pekin Duckling

If it quacks like a duck, chances are it's a duck! This yellow duckling is a beautiful Pekin duckling. Pekins originated in China in the 1800s and are now one of the most popular duck breeds. The delightful yellow coloring of the Pekin duckling changes to a bright white coloring on an adult duck. Most Pekin ducks do not fly.

Duckling Fun Fact

The classic 1933 children's book The Story about Ping *tells the tale of a baby Pekin duckling who wanders away from his family. The book follows Ping's adventures on the Yangtze River in China, and Ping finally rejoins his family for a happy ending.*

Colts and Fillies

Foals love to play! These foals are eight weeks old. A female foal is called a filly, and a male foal is called a colt. Colts tend to be more rambunctious than fillies, as exhibited in this photo. The colt on the right is rearing, while the filly on the left is pinning her ears back and saying, "Stop that!"

Foal Fun Fact
Two fillies that are pastured together often play chasing games where they run races around the field. Two colts that are pastured together play much rougher games than fillies. Colts play games that involve lots of "play" biting and rearing at each other.

Toggenburg Goats

Like the Saanen breed, the Toggenburg dairy goat breed originated in Switzerland. It is known as one of the oldest dairy goat breeds, and the first Toggenburgs were imported to the United States prior to 1900. However, unlike some of the other more colorful dairy goat breeds, the Toggenburgs are always brown with white markings.

Goat Fun Fact

This Toggenburg goat kid illustrates the specific facial markings that are found on the Toggenburg breed. Toggenburg goats have white facial stripes that extend down the face from eye to muzzle. They also have white leg markings. Sometimes the markings are a shade of cream, rather than white, but this is not considered ideal.

Baby Rabbits

Baby rabbits are called kits and are born in litters. Generally speaking, smaller rabbit breeds, including dwarf rabbit breeds, typically have fewer kits per litter, while larger breeds have higher numbers of kits in each litter.

Rabbit Fun Fact

The gestation period for rabbits is between 28 and 31 days, with a couple of days of variation on either side. It has been noted that some specific rabbit breeds have slightly longer gestations. Baby rabbits (kits) that are born before 26 days of gestation are less likely to live.

Dairy Cows and Calves

Farmers in commercial dairies often separate newborn calves from their mothers. The cow is then milked twice a day and the milk is processed and sold to dairies. The baby calf is then bottle fed. However, smaller farms with fewer dairy cows often keep the cow and calf together and allow the calf to continue nursing for weeks or months. This calf and its mother are enjoying a peaceful summer's day in the meadow.

Cow Fun Fact

Historically, cows in large pastures have worn bells. They would help a farmer locate a cow that might have wandered away from the herd while grazing in a large pasture. The farmer would be able to easily locate the cow because the bell would jingle each time the cow moved while grazing or walking.

Stars and Stripes and Blazes

Foals have many different types of white markings on their faces. Some have no white at all, and others have a small white spot called a star. A narrow band of white extending from between the eyes down to the muzzle is called a stripe. If the stripe is wider, perhaps touching the eyes and extending over the muzzle, it is called a blaze.

Foal Fun Fact

Researchers have discovered that white markings on horses are somewhat related to the color of the horse. Chestnut horses are more likely to have extensive white markings (wide blazes and high stockings) than bay horses. However, bay horses are more likely to have extensive white markings than black horses.

Rabbits Kits

Rabbit kits are born blind, deaf, and mostly hairless. The kits will live in a nest box for approximately two weeks, and their mother will visit the nest once or twice a day to feed her young. After about 10 days, the kits' eyes will begin to open, and they will begin to venture outside of their nest box, eat solid food, and become more curious and interested in the world.

Rabbit Fun Fact
The baby Rex rabbit pictured here is an excellent example of the distinctive Rex-type fur. Rex fur is typically quite thick and very soft. Some say it feels like velvet, and Rex rabbits have been referred to as Velveteen rabbits.

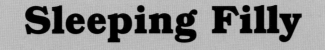

Sleeping Filly

Like most baby animals, foals need plenty of sleep. For their first few weeks, they sleep for several hours each day. They are particularly fond of taking a warm nap in the grass on a sunny day. Once the nap is over, they are back on their feet and ready for more romping and playing!

Foal Fun Fact
Foals can be very choosy about where they take their naps. They seek out soft, grassy places or thickly bedded wood shavings in their stalls. However, many foals like nothing better than to lie down in a large pile of hay and eat it while they rest!

Identifying Calves

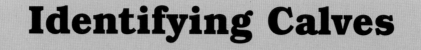

This calf is wearing an identification tag in his ear. This allows the farmer to tell instantly which cow is the calf's mother and also helps the farmer when it comes to keeping records. Over time, the farmer will track the calf's vaccinations and other medical treatments, and later on records will be kept on breeding dates and calving.

Cow Fun Fact

A baby cow is called a calf. An adult male is known as a bull, and an adult female is called a cow. A young cow is called a heifer, and groups of cows are called herds. Calves are born after approximately 285 days of gestation. Cows usually have only one calf at a time and rarely produce twins.

Tabby Kittens

Like all kittens, these two charming tabby-colored kittens are curious about the world and are ready to explore every inch of it together. The tabby coat pattern comes in four varieties: classic, ticked, spotted, and mackerel.

Kittens Fun Fact

A typical tabby marking is what appears to be the letter "M" on the cat's forehead. If you look closely at these two kittens, you will see the "M" marking just above their eyes!

Kittens & Their Friends

Kittens love attention from people and from other animals. They often make friends with other animals in the barn. This kitten has become fast friends with a rabbit. By growing up alongside the other farm animals, kittens learn how to interact with them and learn about life on the farm.

Kitten and Rabbit Fun Fact

Isn't it interesting that baby rabbits are called kits and baby cats are called kittens? They are so different from each other, yet share a similar name. Another baby animal with a similar name is the baby goat, which is called a kid.

Which Came First?

The old saying asks, "Which came first? The chicken or the egg?" While this could be endlessly debated, the bottom line is that baby chicks come from eggs. A female chicken (known as a hen) sits on her nest of eggs (called a clutch) for twenty-one days until the eggs hatch. Eggs can also be hatched by keeping them in a warm incubator. The eggs must be turned frequently if an incubator is used, as a hen will naturally do this when she is sitting on her clutch.

Chicken Fun Fact

In order to hatch, eggs must be kept at a regulated temperature of between 99 and 100 degrees. It's also very important that the humidity in the incubator be kept at approximately 50 to 60 percent until the last few days before hatching, at which time the humidity can be increased to 65 to 70 percent.

Snack Time!

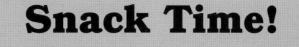

This barn cat has just given birth to a litter of fine, healthy kittens. The kittens will nurse very frequently during the first several days and quickly gain weight and grow strong from the rich milk. Each kitten nurses from a specific teat, which they locate by smell. This prevents arguments between the kittens about where each one will nurse.

Kitten Fun Fact

Kittens are not weaned until after they are about eight weeks old. They begin drinking water and eating solid food prior to this, but they still need the opportunity to nurse from their mother until they are at least eight weeks old. After that time, it's possible to separate the kittens from their mother.

Baa, Baa, Black (or White) Sheep...

This young lamb is calling for its mother, and the sound being made is called bleating. In the first days after a lamb's birth, the ewe and lamb call back and forth so often that they learn to recognize each other's voices, which helps with the bonding process.

Sheep Fun Fact

While cows and horses usually have only one baby at a time, it's very common for ewes (female sheep) to deliver twins or triplets. Some ewes even have quadruplets! Many sheep farmers choose the ewes for their flocks based on their tendency to produce multiple lambs, as that makes the ewe more valuable to the farmer.

Potbellied Pig

A baby pig is called a piglet. This charming piglet is a potbellied pig. An adult male pig is called a boar, and an adult female pig is called a sow. It's interesting to note that when a mare gives birth to a foal, it is called foaling, and when a cow gives birth to a calf, it is called calving. But when a sow gives birth to a litter of piglets, it is not called pigleting. It's actually called farrowing.

Pig Fun Fact

A sow's gestation period is 114 days, which works out to approximately 3 months, 3 weeks, and 3 days, so it is easy to remember. Piglets are born in litters of 10 to 12.

4-H for Fun!

This Red Angus heifer calf is three months old. Red Angus cattle are a color variation on the typical Black Angus breed. This young heifer has been worked with and trained by a young boy for a 4-H project, and she is being prepared for a trip to the county fair.

Animal Fun Fact

Many baby farm animals are exhibited by children at rural county fairs, especially in the 4-H classes. Calves, lambs, kids, and piglets are popular entries, but some children prefer smaller exhibits, such as rabbit kits, chicks, or ducklings. The entries are judged on their condition, breed type, and overall health.

Does and Kids

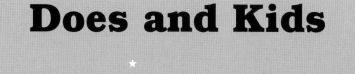

In goat herds, there is often an older doe who is known as the herd queen. The herd queen is a dominant doe who is essentially in charge of the herd and has the distinction of being able to decide where the herd is going to graze and when it's time to move on to a new place. She also is the one who gets to eat first and has the best pick of the available food.

Goat Fun Fact

This African pygmy goat doe is eating hay with her twin kids. The kids watch their mother as she samples the hay, and once she shows them that it's all right to eat, they will join in.

Three Little Ducks

A popular children's song says "Six little ducks that I once knew / Fat ones, skinny ones, fair ones too . . ." And that is absolutely correct! Ducks and ducklings come in all shapes and sizes. The yellow Pekin duckling on the left will grow up to be entirely white and may weigh as much as 10 pounds at maturity. The tall duckling on the right is a Rouen (pronounced roan) and has markings similar to those of a Mallard duck. The Rouen duckling will grow to weigh about 8 pounds. The smaller duckling in the middle is a gray Call duck and will weigh less than 2 pounds at maturity.

Duck Fun Fact

Some duck breeds produce far more eggs per year than other breeds do. A particularly prolific egg producer is the Khaki-Campbell breed of duck. A female Khaki-Campbell duck can produce over 300 eggs each year!

Alpine Goat

Also known as the French Alpine goat, the Alpine is a dairy goat breed that originated in Switzerland, as did the Saanen and the Toggenburg breeds. The Alpines are medium-sized goats that are not as small as the Toggenburg but not as large as the Saanen. Male Alpine goats are noted for having very prominent beards.

Goat Fun Fact

Alpine goats are found in many different colors with a variety of markings, and the distinctive Toggenburg markings are discouraged in the Alpine breed. Often an Alpine is two distinct colors, one color on the front half of the goat and a second color on the other half.

Healthy Chicks

Baby chicks require certain conditions in order to thrive and stay healthy. This means that they must be kept warm and out of the wind and rain. Baby chicks do not need access to food or water until they are three days old, but once the water source is provided, it's important to make sure that it is a safe watering system so that the baby chicks do not drown.

Chick Fun Fact

Many breeders vaccinate their baby chicks at one day of age to protect them against Marek's disease. Because there is no cure for Marek's, it's very important that the chicks are given protection to prevent them from catching the disease.

Calves

There are two basic types of cows: dairy and beef. Dairy breeds include the very popular black-and-white Holstein, the attractive Jersey, and the fawn-colored Guernsey. Beef breeds include the unique Scottish Highland, as well as the popular Angus.

Cow Fun Fact

An average Holstein dairy cow can produce over 20,000 pounds of milk each year. An exceptional Holstein cow can produce over 60,000 pounds of milk in a year. It's no wonder that they are the breed most often chosen for dairy farms!

How Are Ewe?

Adult male sheep are known as rams, and adult female sheep are called ewes. A baby sheep is called a lamb, and lambs are differentiated by gender by calling a male lamb a ram lamb and a female lamb a ewe lamb. A group of sheep is called a flock.

Sheep Fun Fact

As with so many baby animals, lambs love to play! This one is running quickly to rejoin the other members of the flock that are grazing across the field. Sheep are equipped with a very strong natural desire to always remain with their flock.

Mouse Control!

Farms love cats and cats love farms, and troublesome rodents provide the reason for this mutual admiration. Farmers benefit from barn cats because they help keep the rodent population under control, and cats love helping with this important job! This grey kitten is four months old and already learning her job.

Cat Fun Fact

Barn cats sometimes watch for their prey from high locations, and this kitten has climbed up on an outdoor table to watch what's going on below. Some adult barn cats can be a bit wild and unapproachable, but young kittens can be very curious about humans.

Australian Shepherd

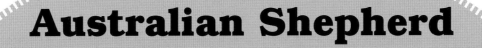

The Australian shepherd, as seen here, is an extremely popular breed on the farm because the breed is hard-working and intelligent. These dogs are easily trained and thrive on having a job to do. And on the farm, there's always a job to do!

Dog Fun Fact

Despite the name, the Australian shepherd does not come from Australia! In fact, the breed was developed in the United States during the 1800s. No one is certain why this American-based breed became known as an Australian shepherd, but some believe that it is related to the merle coloring. Australian immigrants to the United States often had merle-colored dogs, and this may have had an effect on the name of the Australian shepherd breed.

Duck, Duck, Goose

Baby ducks are known as ducklings, while baby geese are known as goslings. An adult male duck is known as a drake, and an adult female duck is known as a duck or a hen. A group of ducks is called a paddle, team, or flock. An adult male goose is called a gander, and an adult female goose is called a goose. A group of geese is called a gaggle.

Duck and Goose Fun Fact

Duck eggs take approximately 28 days to hatch, while goose eggs take up to 35 days. Female ducks are quite protective of their newly hatched ducklings and don't like having other ducks nearby.

Piglets

If you've ever heard the term "runt of the litter," you might be interested to know that it comes from the pig pen. A piglet is considered a runt if it weighs less than 2 pounds at birth. Subsequently, a smaller, weaker piglet can get pushed around by stronger and larger litter mates, resulting in less opportunity to get a share of the sow's milk. Sometimes, runts must be bottle fed to increase their milk consumption.

Pigs Fun Fact

It is recommended that piglets should continue nursing from their mother until they have reached at least 12 pounds. Some farmers prefer to wean them a bit earlier, but it is better for the piglets if they are allowed to nurse for longer periods. This pig is eating pig weed.

A Very Special Rabbit

These unique baby rabbits are Champagne d'Argents. They are a French breed whose name means "Silver Rabbit from Champagne." These rabbits have been bred in France for many years, and some sources say as early as 1631. The first Champagne d'Argent rabbits were brought to the United States in 1912 and called Champagne Silver or French Silver. The breed remained very rare in this country for many years.

Rabbit Fun Fact

There is a very specific coloring that is required in the Champagne d'Argent breed. They should be the color of old silver—a mixture of white, blue, and black—with a darker "butterfly" pattern on the nose. Any yellow tinge or coloring on the body of the rabbit is a serious defect.

Hens and Chicks

Don't get too close! Like most animal mothers, hens are very protective of their babies. These young chicks are being watched by their mother, and she is keeping an eye out for anyone or anything that might bother her babies.

Chick Fun Fact

Chicks are found in many different colors, as shown here. There are many different breeds of chickens, including Araucana, Cochin, Rhode Island Red, Leghorn, Plymouth Rock, Silkie, and Cornish.

Puppies on the Farm

Who doesn't love a puppy? Whether they grow up to be herding dogs, livestock guardians, watch dogs, or cattle dogs, a puppy on the farm is always a bright spot of happiness. Even though the immediate job for a puppy is to be cute and adorable, he or she has a lifetime of work and service ahead if raised on a farm.

Puppy Fun Fact

Puppies are known for being mischievous and curious. This means that puppies on the farm need particular attention because there are so many things that a curious puppy can get into on a farm. They must be carefully watched to make sure that they don't get themselves into trouble.

Goats and Horns

This Nigerian dwarf kid has horns that are just starting to emerge. Some goat breeds are hornless (polled), while other breeds have horns. Many goat kids are disbudded when they are a few days old, preventing their horns from emerging.

Goat Fun Fact

Some goat owners prefer that their baby goats' horns be disbudded for safety. They don't want the goats to inadvertently injure one another (or a human) with their horns. However, some owners believe that the horns are very important to the goat, as they help prevent injury to the goat's skull.

Barn Cats

These playful tabby kittens were raised in the barn, so they are quite at home playing in the hay, climbing on things, and getting into mischief. These kittens are also very familiar with the milking stool and love to wait around for handouts from an obliging cow!

Cat Fun Fact

"Tabby" is not a breed, it's a coat pattern that can occur on a cat of any color. These cute kittens exhibit the tabby coat pattern of stripes intermixed with a base coat color.

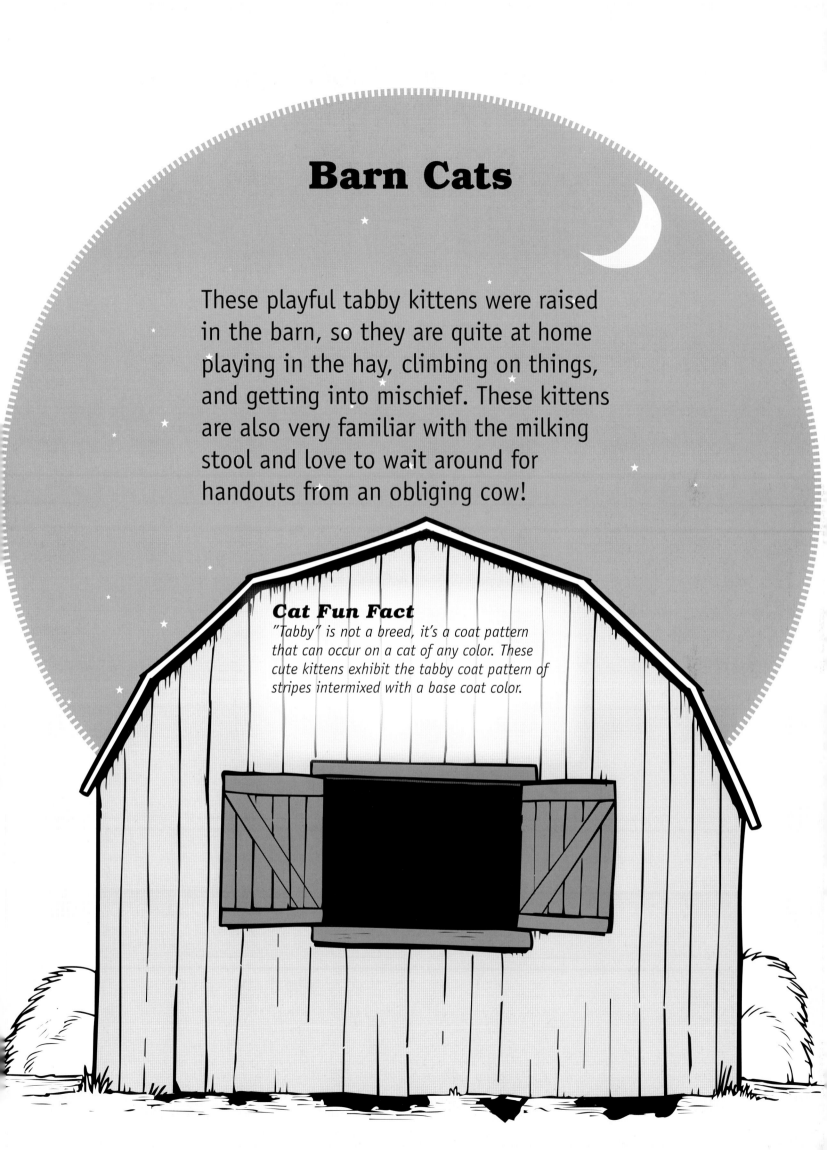

Herding Dogs

The American Kennel Club recognizes twenty breeds in its herding dogs group. These breeds include Australian shepherds, Border collies, collies, Australian cattle dogs, Old English sheepdogs, Welsh corgis, and Shetland sheepdogs. These intelligent and courageous breeds are often found on farms.

Dog Fun Fact
The skills and capabilities of herding dogs can be tested at a competition called a stock dog trial. Highly trained dogs compete for titles and prizes by herding animals, including sheep and ducks, through a course. Each dog is scored individually, and the points are calculated by the judge based on the dog's placing and the number of competitors.

Welsh Mountain Pony

This adorable chestnut foal is a Welsh mountain pony. Her ancestors came from the mountains of Wales. Today Welsh mountain ponies are used for riding and driving, and they are particularly suited for use as a child's pony, due to their small size (less than 12.2 hands or 50 inches).

Foal Fun Fact
Welsh mountain ponies are noted for being the most beautiful native pony breed in the world. They are found in many colors, including black, brown, bay, chestnut, grey, buckskin, and palomino, but the most common colors are grey and chestnut.